God in You: A Conversation (Flower Edition)

2nd Printing

Published by Nesting Tree Books: nestingtreebooks@gmail.com

Illustration & Design: Kenneth Crane

Editor: Sue Miholer

ISBN: 978-0-9839333-4-2

Printed in the United States of America.

GOD *in* YOU

A Conversation

John Stumbo

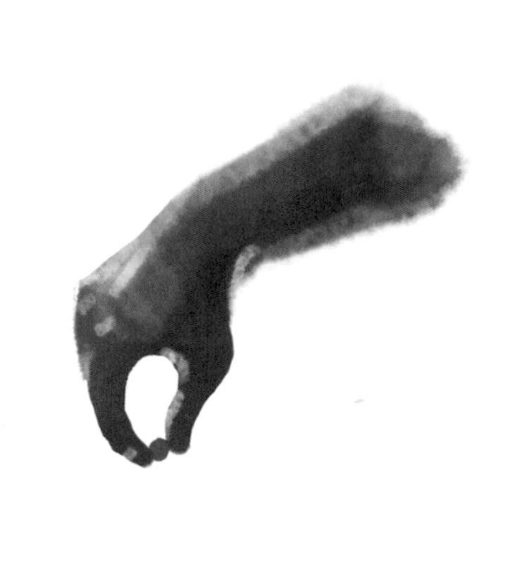

I am aware that God exists.

I believe that you are too.

Deep down,

perhaps buried under a lifetime of pain and unanswered questions,

somewhere within your soul,

you know:

There is a God.

I'm not going to try to prove to you that He exists.

I don't think I have to.

I think you already know.

You may be ignoring Him,
or running from Him.
You may love Him
or hate Him.
You may think He's wonderful
or frightful.
You may not know what to think of Him,
or you may not think of Him at all.

Without faith it is impossible to please God,
because anyone who comes to Him
must believe that He exists . . .
(An Early Jewish Christian)

But of this you can be sure:

God exists.

He's real.

The intimacy of relationships,
the intensity of emotions,
the intricacy of creation,
the immensity of space
all point to
Someone
beyond us,
who is
greater than us.

We're not alone in this world . . .

never have we been,

never were we intended to be.

One thing about God that people seem to miss
is that God is writing a long story.
In this story He offers to make His home with us.
That was the whole point from the beginning
(as in the Garden of Eden beginning).
God created man and woman to be in *relationship* with Him.

We messed up the story line very quickly, of course.

But, our failure to follow

—even our rejection of Him—

is not enough to stop Him.

The long story continues of the God who welcomes us—
including the strays and stubborn holdouts.

Think of it this way:
The God of all eternity has been having a conversation
with you.
He's been there all your life,
desiring your attention,
your affection,
your allegiance,
your heart.

In fact,

He'd like to make a place just for you

in his forever home

called Heaven.

I get tired of company in my house after three days,

but God invites us into His home

for days unending.

Amazing.

His conversation with us is one of love
in all of love's complex dimensions.
In His love He warns,
rebukes,
blesses,
grieves with us,
laughs with us,
calls the best out of us, and
never leaves or abandons us.

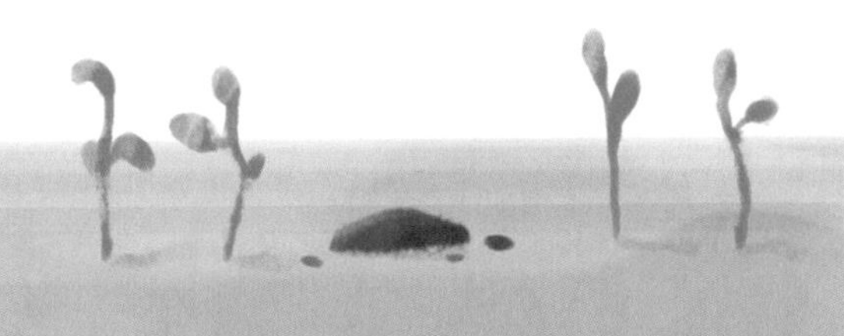

What we do to Him,
on the other hand,
is another issue.

We've been known to be very upset
when He doesn't come through for us as we'd expect.
If I were God,
I would have never let that happen!
This is really quite a silly thing to say
because, of course, we are not God
and have absolutely no idea
what it would be like to be God.

There is one God.

It's not us.

This is a good thing.

Rather than the foolishness
of conjecturing what we would do if we were God,
perhaps we'd be wiser
to get to know the God who exists.
And the God who exists
has been seeking to reveal Himself to us.
This is His nature.
This is who He is:
A relational God
who wants to be known.
Yes, even by people like us.

This, of course, is the whole point of Jesus coming to this world.
The God who made this world
didn't give up on it . . .
even though we have a consistent history
of making a major mess of things.
Rather than rejecting us,
He chose to reach out to us
through Jesus.

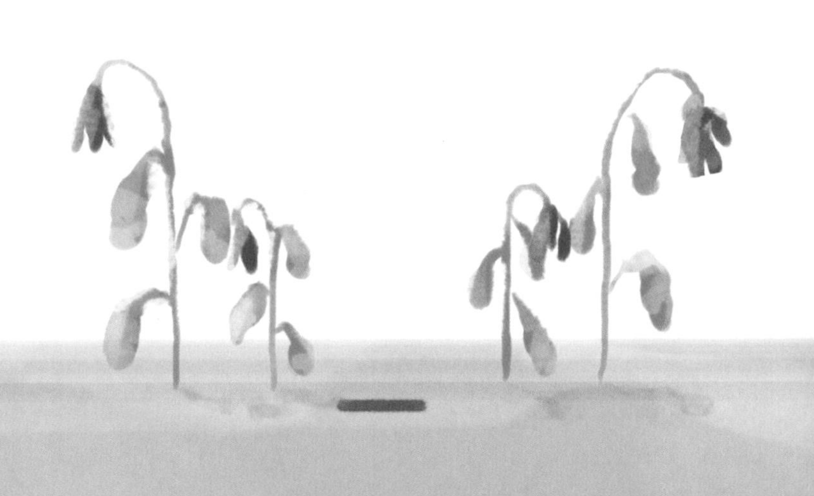

Jesus Himself told us why He came into this world:

To seek and save the lost

were His words.

He didn't come to start a

product line

or political party.

Believe it or not,

He didn't even come to start a religion.

But He did come to show us what God is like
and how we might spend eternity with Him in Heaven.
He did come to warn us that religion could damn you
just as thoroughly as about anything else.
And, He came to die.
Odd, isn't it?
In fact, the whole story of Jesus is
strange,
wild,
and literally
"out of this world."

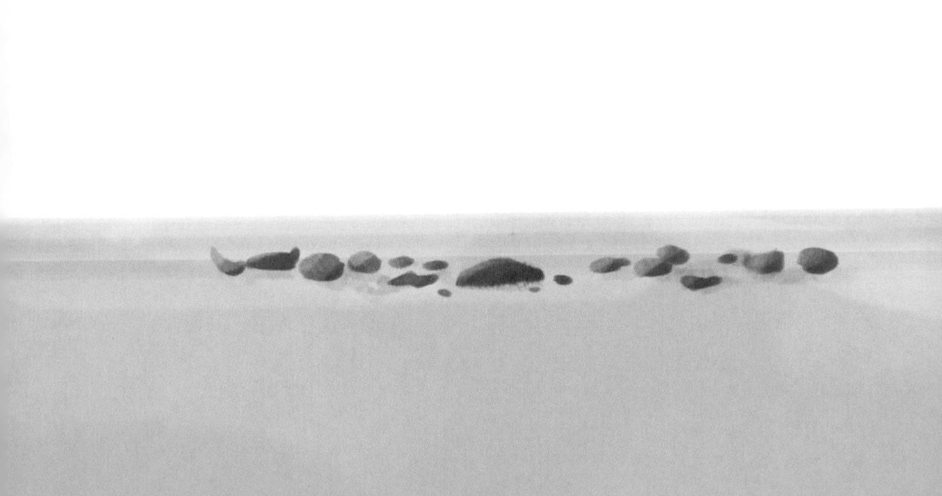

Jesus made the claim that He actually left Heaven
to come to this earth
for the express purpose of dying for our sin.
He claimed that His Father, God,
sent Him here for that very reason.
We, the human race,
in this rare instance
were happy to comply with God's plan.
We killed Jesus.
We nailed Him to a crossbar,
stood around watching as He suffered,
and mocked Him the whole time.

We didn't understand that He was
pierced for our wickedness
and crushed for our sinfulness.
We didn't have eyes to see
that it was *our* punishment He carried.
He bore no wrongdoing of His own in His death
and couldn't bear to have us die in our sin.

Sin.

We're pretty good at missing God's ideals,

doing our own thing,

wanting our own way,

and trying to run our own lives.

We'd rather not have anyone tell us what we can or cannot do—

even God.

But some of us have admitted that this isn't working too well for us.

We admit that we need a Savior.

We want a Savior.

We're lost without a Savior.

Some people view this *lost without a Savior* talk as "weak."
That's understandable.
In fact, it's true.
We're admitting we *are* weak:
too weak to live the life we really want to live,
too weak to love like we really want to love,
too weak to change what we want to change;
and all of this makes us horribly unqualified
for a perfect place like Heaven.

But in this place of weakness,
as we come to Jesus Christ to save us,
we discover an incredible opportunity waiting for us:
an opportunity to be deeply changed
by such exquisite gifts as grace, forgiveness, hope, and peace.

Don't underestimate the power of those gifts.
Divine gifts such as grace, forgiveness, hope, and peace
can break through the hardest heart.
Like a sprout arising out of a crack in the concrete,
the power of new life is beautiful.
Water that sprout and it can grow into a mighty tree,
shattering the former hardness
and replacing it with abundance.

You may think I'm just speaking poetically now
but I tell you, it's real.
Jesus—the Savior—has changed hearts
in the most unexpected places:
prison cells,
cancer wards,
locker rooms,
concentration camps,
fraternity houses,
churches,
kitchens,
fishing boats,
and on that list goes.

No person
in any place
is outside
the reach
of His
life-changing
love.

The

arms

of

the Christ, who stretched out on

the cross, extended wide enough

to

embrace

even

you

and

me.

Please don't misunderstand.
I'm *not* asking you to become a Christian,
if by "Christian" you mean someone who
is aligned with a certain political party,
listens to a certain type of music,
goes to a certain type of church,
or wears a certain type of clothing.

I'm not asking you to embrace all things "Christian."
I certainly don't.
Often what is done under the Christian banner
embarrasses or angers me.
Do you feel the same?
Much that happens
in the name of Christ today
doesn't represent Him very well.

And, this has been going on for a very long time.
"Christian" history is
scandaled and schismed
warred and warped
with stories that bring His name shame.
Proof, I guess,
that even "saints" need a Savior.

I certainly do.
I, for one,
am happy to go on record as saying
that I don't want to stand before God
as my own defense.

Can you imagine the kinds of questions
God might ask us someday?
What did you do with the life I gave you?
How freely did you forgive?
Did you love others as thoroughly as you loved yourself?
Did you care about the things I care about?
Were you perfect as I am perfect?

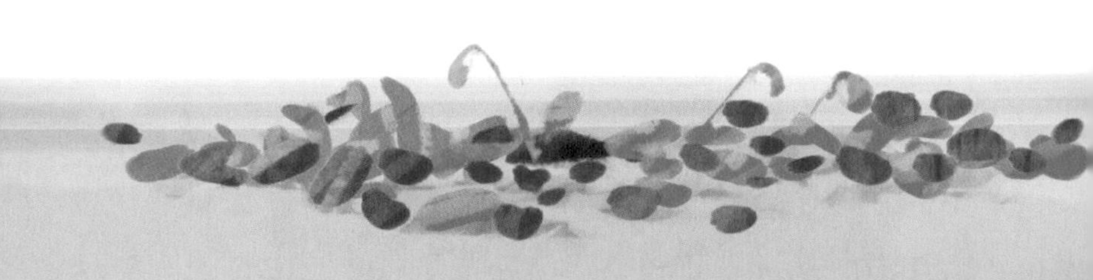

I don't know if God will ask me those exact questions.

But, I do know this:

He has every right and reason to.

He's God.

We're His creation.

It's appropriate for Him to call us to account.

I'm convinced that your understanding of God will be truer,
and your standing before God will be better,
if you come to know Jesus, the Christ:
The Christ who came from Heaven
and lived on this earth.

Christ.

Christian.

Christianity.

The longer the word gets,

the more confusing it gets.

No, I'm not asking you to embrace everything

represented by the longer words.

I *am* challenging you to embrace the Christ.

If the story is true,
it's truly amazing.
The possibility that Jesus was
unique to the entire human race—
leaving Heaven to come to earth in Mary's womb,
growing up to face life's issues just like the rest of us,
yet live sinlessly,
do unprecedented miracles,
teach unparalleled messages,
demonstrate unmatched humility,
die in unimaginable dishonor,
rise from the grave in imperishable life,
and promise to return to earth in uncontestable authority—
is quite a story,
don't you think?

But it's more than a story.

It's an invitation:

an invitation to

repentance,

relationship,

rebirth.

It's an invitation to get to know God
as you've never known Him before.
It's an invitation to experience forgiveness
and to place your life on a new path—
a path that leads to better places
than you've been leading yourself.
It's an invitation to receive a new Spirit,
His.

If I'm at all right that

the God of all eternity is having a conversation

with you . . .

that He's been there all your life,

desiring your attention,

affection,

allegiance,

and your heart.

If this is true,

then "the ball is in your court."

It's your move.

When Jesus walked this earth He announced,

Repent, for the Kingdom of Heaven is near.

He wasn't impressed by the guy who bragged,

God, I thank you that I'm not like other men . . . those losers!

But He was pleased with the one

who confessed with deep emotion,

God, have mercy on me, a sinner.

Later followers of Christ would declare,

Draw near to God and He will draw near to you.

Wash your hands, you sinners,

and purify your hearts, you double-minded,

and

Humble yourselves under God's mighty hand.

They also wrote,

If we confess our sins, He is faithful and just to forgive us our sins,

and

If we are in Christ, we are new creations.

God has done

and keeps doing

His part.

It's your turn.

What will your response be to Him?

He's been speaking to you.

Isn't it time to start listening to Him . . . and responding?

"Well, okay . . ."

You might be thinking.

"But, I'm not sure where to start."

Faith is the starting point.

Maybe you are ready to say to Him something like this:

God, I believe You exist.

I believe You are real.

I believe in You.

If your heart agrees, go ahead and say these words out loud.

Speak your faith:

God, I believe You exist.

I believe You are real.

I believe in You.

The next affirmation presses our faith a little further,

God, I believe that You are good.

I don't understand You, but I do believe that

Your goodness contains all the things that I need . . .

things like grace and truth,

forgiveness and love.

Is something in your heart saying, "*YES*"?

Then speak out those words.

You are now joining the conversation that
God has been having with you for so long.
As your heart continues to lean in,
this will be life-changing.

If you've stated your belief that God exists,

that He is good

and

that you need His good work in your life,

doesn't the next response naturally follow?

Forgive me!

I don't deserve a relationship with You.

I don't deserve to know You.

I don't deserve to be welcomed into Your heaven-home.

Forgive me for how I've treated You . . . and others . . . and myself.

Confession feels healthy once it starts to flow.
Let more words of your own arise.
For a lifetime we've carried the weight of guilt—
or tried to outrun its nagging voice.
There's a better way!
You are discovering it!
It's called repentance:
Admitting that we've been wrong
and turning away from that behavior
to the kind of life that our Maker intended for us to live.

Repent, for the Kingdom of Heaven is near.

(Jesus)

It's His kindness that leads us to repentance.

(The Apostle Paul)

God, I want to be done leading my own life.
I want to be done pretending I'm good enough.
I want YOU and everything You have for me.

I have come that you might
have life abundant.

(Jesus)

These are the kinds of prayers that delight God.
This is the kind of response Jesus came to produce in us.
This is the entry point to new life.

Come to me all who are weary and I will give you rest.

(Jesus)

Salvation is found in no one other than Jesus,
for there is no other name under heaven given to men
by which we must be saved.

(The Apostle Peter)

What may start to arise next within you is *gratitude*.

Does it feel like the conversation should turn to eager appreciation?

God!

Thank You for sending Jesus to earth!

Thank You that my sin was paid for at the cross!

Thank You that Jesus died for me!

Thank You for forgiveness!

I admit that I'm not good enough to enter heaven on my own,

yet I eagerly accept Your offer to give me eternal life.

Thank You for this incredible gift. I receive it!

If your heart has been welcoming this message,
you are joining the conversation that God has been having with you.
No doubt He has much more to say to you
and you have much more to say to Him.
He's eager for your relationship to deepen at any time.

As you pursue your relationship with God,
you'll increasingly find that you are living a
"God-directed" life rather than a self-directed one.
God will be the One *directing* your life
and
the *direction* of your life will be toward God.

Jesus died for all
that those who live
should no longer live for themselves
but for Him who died for them
and was raised again.
(The Apostle Paul)

This is a complete reversal from the *self*-directed life
we've been living . . .
living for ourselves
and seeking to be in charge of ourselves.
Now, we live for Him and by Him.

Remain in Me and I will remain in you.
(Jesus)

Nothing in all creation can separate us
from the love of God in Christ Jesus.
(The Apostle Paul)

Never will I leave you.
Never will I forsake you.
(God)

God living in you,

and

you living in Him.

Crazy? Yes.

Real? Definitely.

Only as long as you feel it? Nope.

He's not going anywhere.

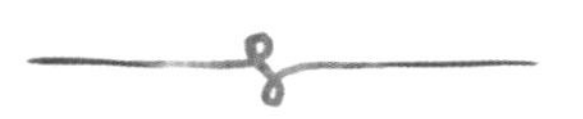

Don't be surprised by the painful trial you now enduring
as though something strange were happening to you.
(The Apostle Peter)

In this world you will have opposition.
Be of good cheer.
I have overcome the world.
(Jesus)

Of course, in all of this we will face opposition.
Forces are at work that don't want you to follow God's path.
You are probably familiar with them already:
Satan and his demons
—at war against all that is good—
attempt to lie to us, rob us, and blind us.
Our own old nature
—the part of us that likes sin—
wants control and whines when it doesn't get it.
The world around us
—with its constant messages and influences—
begs for our attention.
Even some of our family and friends
may not be supportive of the changes they see in us.

In all these things we are more than conquerors
through Jesus Christ our Lord.
(The Apostle Paul)

Greater is He that is in you
than he that is in the world.
(The Apostle John)

But know this:

Greater is He that is in you than anything that can come against you.

Faithful is He who called you and He will keep working in you.

Unfailing is His love. Unending is His mercy.

You are His.

He is Yours.

I soon need to bring this book to a close,
but your conversation with God is just started.
What can I do to continue this conversation . . .
to grow in my relationship with God?
I can't fully answer that,
but I can begin an answer
with ways that God has
strengthened the relationship of
many of His followers through the centuries:

Invite His Holy Spirit to fill every part of you.
Get to know Him better through studying the Bible.
Make your faith public through water baptism.
Share this message with someone you love.
Find community in a Jesus-honoring church.
Welcome a believing friend to walk this journey with you.
Extend the forgiveness that you've received to those who hurt you.
Talk to Him about the issues that concern you.
Become more concerned about the priorities that are on His heart.
Grow deeper in the love that He has for you . . .

I don't think there really is an end to such a list
because there is no end
to our opportunity
to go further
in our relationship with Him.

Warning!

Wrongly understood, such a list
could feel like the
what-I-have-to-do-to-be-good-enough list.

His divine power has given us everything we need
for life and godliness.
(The Apostle Peter)

God is at work in you
to desire and to do His good pleasure.
(The Apostle Paul)

Let's change the picture.

Rather than trying to be good enough for God,

instead think in terms of joining Him in His goodness.

God is the One who is truly good.

He's at work in you.

He will keep working in you.

He's the Initiator.

Our part is to cooperate . . . letting Him *direct* us, remember?

. . . until Christ is formed in you . . .

(The Apostle Paul)

As we learn to follow His direction
—listening, yielding, obeying—
something really cool starts happening:
We start seeing characteristics of Jesus show up in our lives.
Like lush fruit growing on a tree,
God's Spirit wants to produce beautiful qualities in us, such as:
Love, joy, peace, patience, kindness, goodness,
faithfulness, gentleness, and self-control . . .
the very attributes that describe Jesus' life.

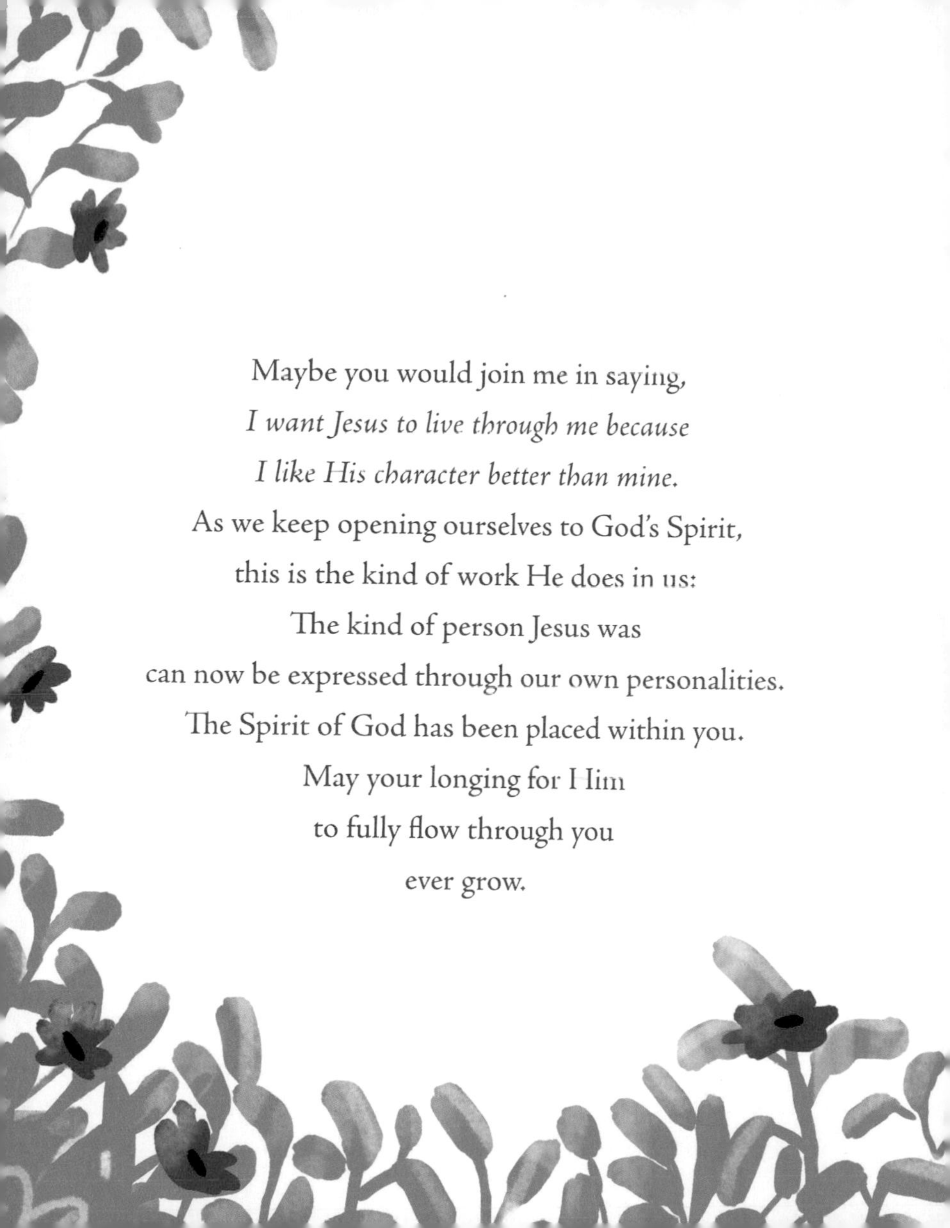

Maybe you would join me in saying,
I want Jesus to live through me because
I like His character better than mine.
As we keep opening ourselves to God's Spirit,
this is the kind of work He does in us:
The kind of person Jesus was
can now be expressed through our own personalities.
The Spirit of God has been placed within you.
May your longing for Him
to fully flow through you
ever grow.

This little book is ending, yet
God's conversation with you is only beginning.
And, so, I encourage you . . .

Without faith it is impossible to please God,
because anyone who comes to Him
must believe that He exists . . .
and that He is a rewarder
of those who diligently seek Him.
(An Early Jewish Christian)

Keep

seeking

the

God

who

seeks

you.

Y
GOD
U

Out of the Father's glorious riches
may He
strengthen you with power in your innermost being,
so that Christ may dwell in your hearts through faith
and that you
—being firmly planted in love—
may know
how wide and long, high and deep
is the
love of Christ
for
you,
and in you
and through you.
May you be filled to overflowing
with everything that the Spirit is and provides.
Amen.

BIBLE REFERENCES CITED

Page	Scripture
8 and 138	But without faith it is impossible to please Him, for he who comes to God must believe that He is, and that He is a rewarder of those who diligently seek Him. *Hebrews 11:6*
37	For the Son of Man has come to seek and to save that which was lost. *Luke 19:10*
43	But He was wounded for our transgressions, He was bruised for our iniquities; The chastisement for our peace was upon Him, and by His stripes we are healed. *Isaiah 53:5*
85	Also He spoke this parable to some who trusted in themselves that they were righteous, and despised others: "Two men went up to the temple to pray, one a Pharisee and the other a tax collector. The Pharisee stood and prayed thus with himself, 'God, I thank You that I am not like other men—extortioners, unjust, adulterers, or even as this tax collector. I fast twice a week; I give tithes of all that I possess.' And the tax collector, standing afar off, would not so much as raise his eyes to heaven, but beat his breast, saying, 'God, be merciful to me a sinner!' I tell you, this man went down to his house justified rather than the other; for everyone who exalts himself will be humbled, and he who humbles himself will be exalted." *Luke 18:9–14*

85 and 104	From that time Jesus began to preach and to say, "Repent, for the kingdom of heaven is at hand." *Matthew 4:17*
87	Draw near to God and He will draw near to you. Cleanse your hands, you sinners; and purify your hearts, you double-minded. *James 4:8* Therefore humble yourselves under the mighty hand of God, that He may exalt you in due time. *1 Peter 5:6*
89	If we confess our sins, He is faithful and just to forgive us our sins and to cleanse us from all unrighteousness. *1 John 1:9* Therefore, if anyone is in Christ, he is a new creation; old things have passed away; behold, all things have become new. *2 Corinthians 5:17*
104	Or do you despise the riches of His goodness, forbearance, and longsuffering, not knowing that the goodness of God leads you to repentance? *Romans 2:4*
106	The thief does not come except to steal, and to kill, and to destroy. I have come that they may have life, and that they may have it more abundantly. *John 10:10*

108 Come to Me, all you who labor and are heavy laden, and I will give you rest.

Matthew 11:28

Nor is there salvation in any other, for there is no other name under heaven given among men by which we must be saved.

Acts 4:12

114 He died for all, that those who live should live no longer for themselves, but for Him who died for them and rose again.

2 Corinthians 5:15

116 Abide in Me, and I in you. As the branch cannot bear fruit of itself, unless it abides in the vine, neither can you, unless you abide in Me. I am the vine, you are the branches. He who abides in Me, and I in him, bears much fruit; for without Me you can do nothing.

John 15:4–5

For I am persuaded that neither death nor life, nor angels nor principalities nor powers, nor things present nor things to come, nor height nor depth, nor any other created thing, shall be able to separate us from the love of God which is in Christ Jesus our Lord.

Romans 8:38–39

Let your conduct be without covetousness; be content with such things as you have. For He Himself has said, "I will never leave you nor forsake you."

Hebrews 13:5

118 Beloved, do not think it strange concerning the fiery trial which is to try you, as though some strange thing happened to you; but rejoice to the extent that you partake of Christ's sufferings, that when His glory is revealed, you may also be glad with exceeding joy.

1 Peter 4:12–13

These things I have spoken to you, that in Me you may have peace. In the world you will have tribulation; but be of good cheer, I have overcome the world."

John 16:33

120 Yet in all these things we are more than conquerors through Him who loved us.

Romans 8:37

You are of God, little children, and have overcome them, because He who is in you is greater than he who is in the world.

1 John 4:4

121 He who calls you is faithful, who also will do it.

1 Thessalonians 5:24

130 Grace and peace be multiplied to you in the knowledge of God and of Jesus our Lord, as His divine power has given to us all things that pertain to life and godliness, through the knowledge of Him who called us by glory and virtue,

2 Peter 1:2–3

… it is God who works in you both to will and to do for His good pleasure.

Philippians 2:13

132 … until Christ is formed in you.

Galatians 4:19

133 But the fruit of the Spirit is love, joy, peace, longsuffering, kindness, goodness, faithfulness, gentleness, self-control.

Galatians 5:22–23

143 For this reason I bow my knees to the Father of our Lord Jesus Christ, from whom the whole family in heaven and earth is named, that He would grant you, according to the riches of His glory, to be strengthened with might through His Spirit in the inner man, that Christ may dwell in your hearts through faith; that you, being rooted and grounded in love, may be able to comprehend with all the saints what is the width and length and depth and height—to know the love of Christ which passes knowledge; that you may be filled with all the fullness of God.

Ephesians 3:14–19

ABOUT THE AUTHOR

John and his lifetime bride, Joanna, are pleased to be the parents of three and grandparents of two (so far). Joanna claims Ohio as home, John Minnesota, but currently they live in Colorado where John serves as president of a Christian ministry. He has earned degrees in Bible, theology and leadership. His decades as an active sportsman often found him with hiking boots, running shoes, tennis rackets, or fishing poles. A sudden illness disabled him from pursuing such activities for a few years, but he's back (a little slower now) in pursuit of the next trail, mountaintop or lake. More information is available at johnstumbo.com

ABOUT THE ILLUSTRATOR

Kenneth Crane is a freelance artist, having earned separate degrees in both graphic design and illustration. He currently lives in his native state of Colorado. Employed as a full-time graphic designer for a nationwide, nonprofit organization, he has learned the finer points of working with head, heart, and hand. And itching for the outdoors, Kenneth is also a long-distance runner and avid mountaineer, gathering inspiration from these adventures to fuel future projects. His work can be viewed at kennethcrane.com.

ALSO BY JOHN STUMBO

An Honest Look at a Mysterious Journey

Life suddenly "turned" for pastor and ultra-marathon runner John Stumbo at age 47. A mysterious illness left him bedridden for 77 days and unable to swallow for more than a year. John and his wife, Joanna, tell their story in a manner that is authentic, moving, insightful, and, at times, humorous.

In the Midst: Treasures from the Dark

With a feeding tube hanging from his stomach, a disease ravaging his muscles, and questions raging in his soul, John Stumbo committed to be transparently honest. He also resolved to write about his experience—not only for others to read but also as a means of understanding what he truly believed in the midst of his crisis.